Sandw... Wraps

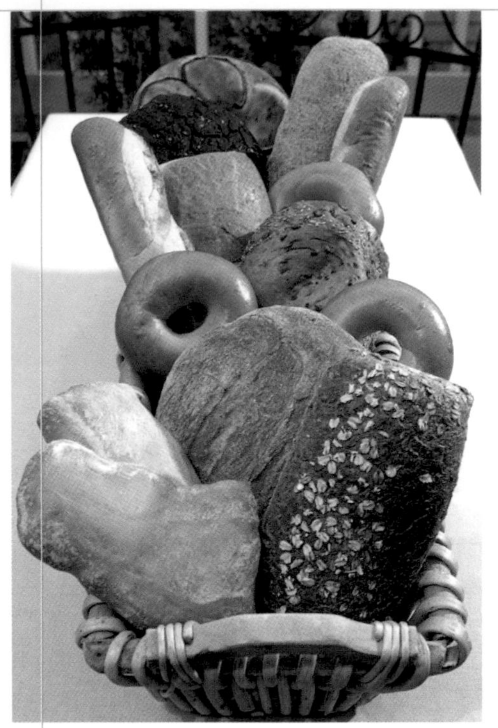
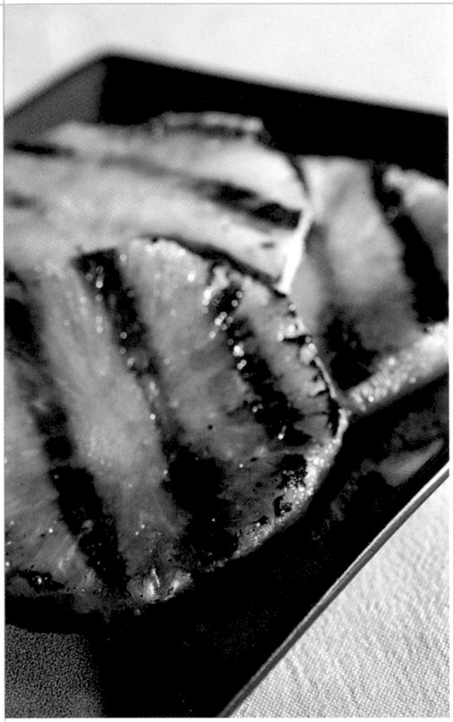
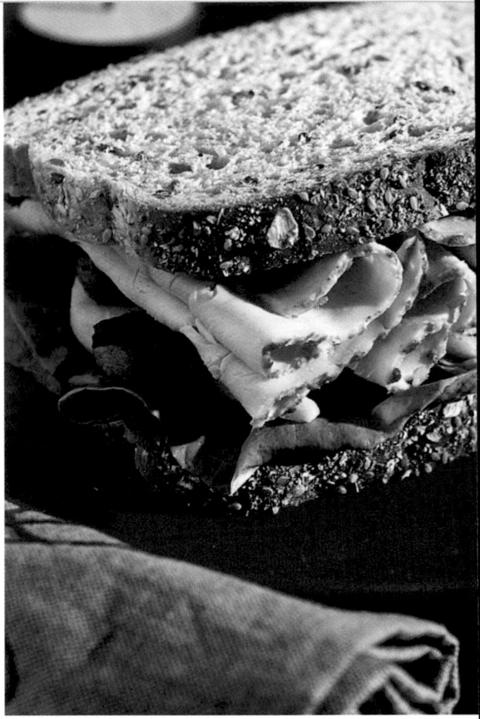
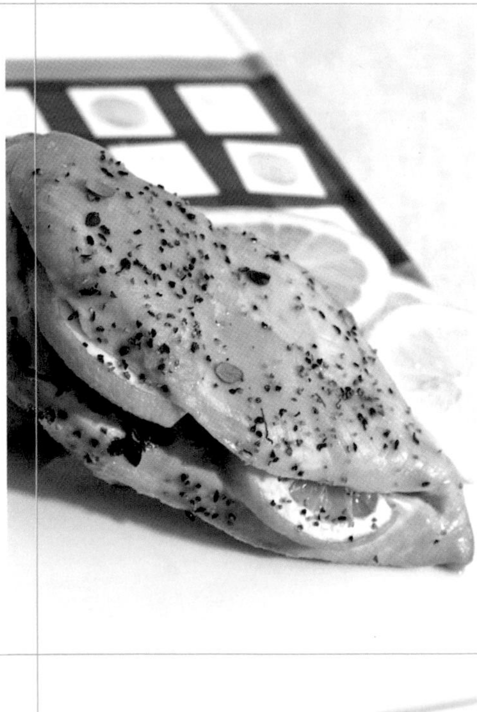
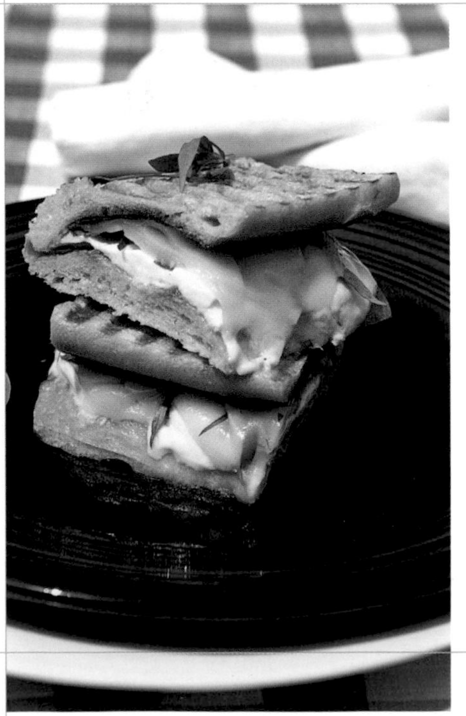
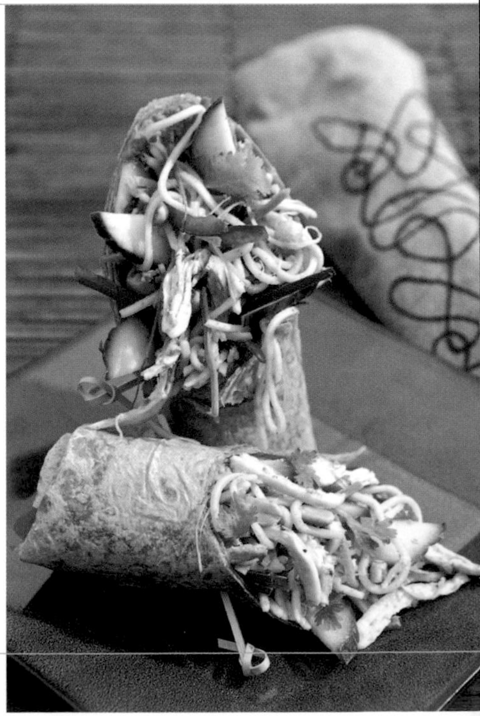